T

Pipe Dreams... 4

Early May...7

The Other Side of Jericho............................8

Bad Boy...12

Between You, Me, and Kinsey 15

Dream Encyclopedia...................................19

The Ones That Chose Water........................20

Tough Love Poem To My Mother..................22

I Remember Climbing High...........................25

Rambo Renegades..26

Dust Bowl...29

On Breaking Clouds....................................32

Writer's Block...33

Waterslide..34

Acknowledgements

I would like to thank several people who helped this collection come together.

First, I'd like to thank KT Herr and Kaira Williams for their thorough critiques, edits, and proofreading of these pieces. I would also like to thank Justin Razmus for the beautiful cover art, and Eirann Betka for the artistic formatting. Also, a big thank you to everyone who has been a fan or supported my art in any way. A special thank you to my partner, confidant, and the love of my life, Taylor Roberts. Finally, a very big thank you to Fable The Poet who saw potential in me and continues to push me every single day to reach that potential and actualize my artistic visions.

Introduction

This collection of poems has been a long time coming. Some of these pieces were written seven years ago, and the most recent was finished just a few weeks before I published this book.

Each of them has a dear place in my heart as they represent specific moments in my journey since the time I decided rebellion was my new religion. I hope some of them strike a chord for you at whatever point you may be in your own journey.

-Rachel

Pipe Dreams

I believe in pipe dreams,
in clouds of blue-grey smoke with brilliant silver linings.
I believe in scratch-off lottery tickets,
in two-dollar Cashwords with big pots and impossible odds.
I believe in those fleeting moments of ridiculous hope
when you're worshiping the worn edge
of that Susan B. Anthony coin,
worshiping that friction
and praying for the letter T
because a T
would fucking change
your life
forever.

I believe in hope for the sake of hoping.
I believe in the god of instinct.
I believe in the women locked up at Kent County,
walking the perimeter of the "big pod"
in groups of twos and threes,
walking miles and miles in circles,
walking miles in circles that would
stretch across state lines,
for some of them to coastlines.
If only they could walk outside.

I believe in the god of small things,
in Knock Knock jokes with x-rated punchlines,
in well-weathered faces with deep grooved crow's feet
and even deeper laugh lines.
I believe in getting lost as a pastime,
in criss-crossing double backed map lines.
I believe in remembering the bad times,
the being-grateful-for-what-we-have times.

I believe in Stonewall and the riots of '69
when the bull dykes and drag queens
decided that their bar had been raided-
that they'd been invaded and degraded
for the last time.

When transwarriors whipped off their stilettos
and wielded them against beat cops with billy clubs.
I believe in the beauty of their thick muscles
shifting and sliding beneath sequins and taffeta
as they overturned high top tables,
sending smoking ashtrays
and half-drunk lipsticked beer bottles flying.
I believe in that constant, relentless motion,
that howl of refusal.

I believe in resisting arrest
when being arrested means being
beaten and maimed and raped.
I believe in the kind of rage that silences hate,
in the kind of pride that renounces shame.
I believe in a god of many faces and many names.
I believe in the god of losers, of boozers,
of mutts and of tramps and of wannabes.
I believe in a god that says, "Try me".

I believe in hopeless cases, in dead end races.
I believe in the god of possibility.
I believe in myself.

I believe in myself the way that children
with bath towels tied around their necks
believe they are heroes.

I believe in myself the way that oil slicks
in empty parking lots believe they are rain-
bows.

I believe in the god of rationalization,
of delirium and delusion.
I believe in the god of certainty.
I believe that nothing is certain.
I believe in the god of contradiction.
And this is the god that rules me.

I believe in mutiny,
in manipulating reality.
I believe in belief for the sake of believing,
in exhaling clouds of blue-green smoke
with brilliant silver linings...
I believe in pipe dreams.

Early May

Today is a day for catching birds bare-handed.
For reaching into the sky with expectant,
full-stretched fingers and bringing them down again,
enclosed around feathered defiance—
desperate wings and hollow bones,
holding her just for a moment.

Today is a day for releasing prisoners from gentle fists.
For feeling restrained power suddenly burst forth,
leap from open palms and take flight,
disappearing into a world just out of reach,
treetops and rooftops and telephone wires.
Today is a day for catching birds bare-handed.

The Other Side Of Jericho

The human brain is a machine, a complex network,
a starlit series of intricate compartments
interconnected by superhighway synapses,
my gray matter mechanism,
fold upon fold of intellectual potential
flickering like the light of a lingering ghost
asserting its unrelenting presence.
There is a myth that we only use 20%
of our full brain capacity,
but I don't think that's true and if you ask me that's just an excuse
for apathy and maybe that's why everybody
laughs at me.

Because I use humor as a defense mechanism.

Because we all fall short,
but at least I know my place in this organism.

I know that life is chaos, is ridiculous beauty;
I know mutation creates diversity,
that consciousness is random,
is fractal absurdity.

And I want to laugh.

I want to laugh like Sarah laughed
when the angel told her
that her ninety year old womb
bore life.

I want to howl with laughter until I weep
in gratitude for my ability to be,
to think, to analyze, to speak.
Because my brain is a miracle machine.

And I am an inadequate vessel
struggling to seize what has been laid before me,
endless possibilities, because we all fall short.
And still I regret nothing,
not a single wasted moment
because I chose it
and all time is now, is future, is history,
is constantly rising and setting,
the hot sun burning my back as I wander,
the hot sand burning the bottoms of my bare feet.
And I would wander through this desert
for another forty years
as long as it brought me to my promise,
me to my knees
and back to my burning, bleeding feet
to the place where I now stand
on the other side of Jericho from my dream.

And I want to scream.

I want to scream like Joshua screamed.
I want to be red faced and holy.
I want to scream until my voice becomes a howl
no human ear can hear.
I want to scream until the walls I have built
unimaginably high, inconceivably thick, that mortar and brick,
begins to crumble and split
by the force of my sound.

I want to scream like Joshua screamed.
I want to be that desperate and unleashed.
I want to scream against everything
that separates me from me.
I want to scream until heaven has no choice
but to answer
because I want what was promised to me.
I want to scream until inactive synapses
begin to crackle and finally to fire
because human will is physical, is palpable
and anything is possible
because mountains are made of the same grain
as mustard seeds,
because the god in us can bury great cities
under even greater seas

because all time is now
is future, is history
and we are all a part
of this ridiculous reality
and the breath in my lungs
is the same cosmic wind
that brought this world to be

and it is finally time to awaken
the god that sleeps
in the deepest
part of me.

Bad Boy

When I grow up I wanna be a bad boy.

I wanna be taken away kicking and screaming.
I wanna be James Dean on a chopper and leaning
into the curve of a new kind of rebellion.

When I grow up I wanna hold amber glass bottles
loosely by the necks.
I wanna smoke Marlboro Reds
and I wanna throw those amber glass bottles up against
your concrete walls of masculinity.

I wanna be reckless, shirtless, working in the sun.
I wanna be sweaty and dirty and I wanna feel that hunger
deep in my sex. I wanna be hard and cold,
a distant lover, the kind you can't
take home to mother.

When I grow up I wanna be a bad boy.
I wanna throw punches and barstools.
I wanna be boozed and bruised.
I wanna wear my wounds on my body
and not on my psyche. I wanna have black eyes
and tattoos and scars that tell stories.

When I grow up I wanna be a bad boy.
I wanna go 90 down your New Deal highway
and not wear a helmet just to dare your road to shake me.
I wanna crash through your barriers, collide with controversy.
I wanna leave permanent treadmarks all the fuck over
your constructed history.

When I grow up I wanna be a bad boy.

Now I'm all grown up and I'm no brooding badass.
I'm just a tattooed jackass
with C-cup tits
and curvy hips
and my mother thinks that I'm gay because she thinks that I think
that I'm not pretty.

And I might not be, but goddammit I know
that I'm sexy.
Now I'm all grown up and I've got muscle,
but I thought I'd be stronger.
Nothing has killed me quite yet, but I can't take this
much longer.
Now I'm all grown up
I'm just a scared little girl
and I'm still
dreaming that I'm James Dean on a chopper and leaning
into the curve of a new kind of rebellion.

And I might be a fool
but I am hoping
that around that bend
there's a world that will welcome me.

Now I'm all grown up and I
know that my delusions will never be
reality, but I'm still throwing my little girl fists up
against your concrete walls of blind regularity
and my knuckles are bleeding,
I'm not making any dents, but at least I am trying.

Now I'm all grown up and
I'm not a bad boy,
but I'm sure as hell not a lady and your
All American ideas of normalcy
will never ever fucking confine me.

Now I'm all grown up and I might be a wannabe.
I'm no James Dean and I don't own a chopper.
And yes I do have a cause,
I'm skirting the limits of your laws
and I am riding even further into
my own kind of rebellion.

Between You, Me, and Kinsey

If you kissed me you'd probably like it,
but you wouldn't taste cherry chapstick,
and to be honest, I'd rather just skip it.
Because I don't really feel like being anybody else's
Katy-Perry-inspired college experiment
because in the morning you'll still
swear by the dick
and I'll still be the one who gets stared at in public
because I'll never be a lipstick.
I'll never quite fit

in that tight little box
that we call female.

And three years from now
you'll marry and settle down
and no one will know you're not really
a *one* on the Kinsey Scale
and I'll still be talking shit
about the Disney fairytales
and cursing myself because even I failed
at becoming the role model that girls like me
never had

because instead of making integrity my priority
I let myself become your experience in novelty
and for some reason that was hot to me.

And while you were driving back to your boyfriend's house,
I was bragging to my friends that I got up your skirt
and under your blouse.
And while you were walking through your boyfriend's front door
and creeping across his linoleum floor
I was pretending to sleep and to believe
that I will be more than a punchline in the stories
that you will tell about your
"crazy college days" when you are old and boring.

But this is not a joke.
This is my life.

And I know that life's not fair
and that complaining won't change it,
but it's not. Fucking. Fair.

Why should you get to have sizzling sex and skip the stigma?
Get your brains fucked out
then wipe your mouth
and return to your seat of privilege?
And I'm the one who's taking advantage?

It's hot because it's taboo and taboo is trendy
until it fucks with your real life and you have to defend
your
straight identity.
Do you have any idea what I lost
when I rejected that dichotomy?
My friends. My faith. And damn near everything.

And I would lose it all again
and it would still be worth it to me.

Even to be stretched so thin across this skewed
spectrum of expression and sexuality,
to be moved down one more drawer
in the filing cabinet of social hierarchy.

But I am not confined or defined that easily.

And to be honest, getting stared at at the Jenison Meijer
doesn't really bother me
because the fact that you're so boring
you find me interesting
is pretty damn entertaining,
but can you please stop teaching
your children to hate me?

Because when your sheltered little girls grow up
it will only make them want to fuck me.

And I'm over it.
But even as I say this
I'm afraid I'll scare away a potential lay
because at the end of the day
old habits die hard and while I don't like the game,
I can't help but play.

Especially when you smile and giggle
and walk my way
then lean in and whisper,
"If I weren't straight…"
If only you knew,
that's what they all say
right before shit
is about to get
pretty damn gay.

Dream Encyclopedia

She looks up the meanings of our dreams in the morning,
searching symbols, keywords, summaries.

Threatened by a Knife means she's feeling
unsettled, insecure, exposed.

Multiple Sex Partners means I'm feeling
physically detached, bored, dissatisfied.

She asks if I ever come
in my dreams, in my sleep.

I rinse a blue cereal bowl,
slide it into the top rack of the dishwasher
and ask: in hers does she ever bleed?

The Ones That Chose Water

I wonder what she was thinking when she was driving along that beach, the pregnant woman in the minivan with her three kids in the back. I wonder what she was thinking in those moments before the pane of glass in her pressure chamber mind cracked. When, like a brake line between the blades of a pair of wire cutters, something in her soul snapped. And I'm wondering if she wishes she could take the hard right she made into the ocean back. But it's two hours later and she still hasn't said a word since the minivan and the heavy surf made impact. To me, she'll always be walking back to shore with that dazed look in her eye. Her clothes will never dry. She will always be salt-stained and soaked from the waist down. She's just another name and face now. Just a few more front pages to grace now because she's joined the ranks of the Andrea Yates, the Diane Downs, and the Susan Eubanks, dodging lethal injection needles and toothbrush shanks. And when I looked up mothers that had killed their children I found myself swimming through names upon names upon names. Leatrice Brewer. Fiona Anderson. Jamie Clutter. And I wonder why so many of them chose water. I suppose there is something about water that seems gentler if not quicker. But blood is supposed to be thicker. Tell that to the rocks at the bottom of the river. Tell it to the fathers. See, I find myself stuck on the ones that chose water, the ones that chose bathtubs and minivans and buried their babes in tomb waters. Mr. Bubble, crystal clear. Murky pond, river, lake, ocean-deep doom waters. White knuckles and blank faces bringing them back to overflowing womb waters, back to where they came from, storks with straining wings flying back to heaven with dripping wet sons and half grown daughters. See, I find myself stuck on the ones that chose water and they say nothing compares to the love of a mother. No, there's nothing in this world like the love of a mother. Nothing quite like the horror of talk about demons and of misguided love with only one solution to offer. No there's nothing in this world like the love of a mother. And this about the ones with pressure chamber minds, the ones who bake cookies with extra chocolate chips and a splash of turpentine, the ones with a pair of wire cutters for every brake line. And they've got the kiddos strapped in tight in the backseat. They've got belts and buckles and child locks with the keys thrown out of reach. They've got deep tubs and strong hands and too many lessons to teach and I can't stop thinking about the pregnant woman on the beach whose children survived. All three were saved and taken to the hospital where the doctors said they were fine. Well, maybe not fine, but they were alive. Still, I wonder if years from now they'll wish they had died instead of living with the memory of what she had tried. I wonder if for them, she will always be standing in that high tide with that empty look in her eyes. I wonder if for them, she will always be pregnant and lost and salt-stained from the waist down, standing in the surf with that look on her face like she's still got the gas pedal down.

Tough Love Poem To My Mother

I used to hang from your words like they were monkey bars
stretching across the stars
in the handle of the Big Dipper, leading me North.
But there is no North among the stars
that are really so far apart
I wouldn't be able to reach the next one anyway.
And there is no momentum
in the vacuum of space that is between us.
And there used to be negative space between us.
I used to live inside of you.
And I remember you telling me that I was breech,
that I was always elbowing your ribcage and kicking your tailbone,
but I was just trying to climb high enough
so I could use your heart for my pillow.
So I could learn the rhythm of life and create one of my own.
And I don't think I've ever understood you
as well as I did before the doctors turned me.
And I remember you telling me
how they placed their hands on either side
of your swollen abdomen, on either side of me
and pushed like you would soon push,
forcing me around, jarring me into the correct position
and that set everything in motion.
You went into labor the next day,
expelling me into their hands
and they laid me on your chest
so I could find your heart again
and you whispered my name

and I struggled to open my eyes so I could match the
voice I'd been hearing in the dark
to your face,
experiencing for the first time the coldness of space,
joining the race that is not so much a moving forward
as it is a slow and steady moving apart.
And I don't think I've ever been as close to you
as I was when I was a toddler,
sitting on your lap and feeling the thump of your heart
on the back of my skull
as you read to me.
The vibration of your voice
resonating in my own chest
and spinning out like a tumbling web,
the aesthetic of love.
It was always the feeling of your words
and not their meaning that I clung to.
And I just wanted to please you.
But I was different.
Unlike my siblings, I lost interest in books.
I was bare chested in the woods,
where sticks were my swords and rocks were grenades
and mud was my war paint.
And when I was eight
you told me I was no longer allowed to go shirtless outside.
I must have had you terrified.
But even twenty years later
all I've ever wanted was validation from you,
not birthday cards with Bible verses and poems you wrote me,
strict stanzas with ABBA rhyme schemes calling me back to God
and to my sacred femininity.   23

You gave me words when all I wanted was for you to just look at me,
even if you couldn't celebrate me, to at least really see me
instead of clinging to a vision of a future redeemed me.
You gave me words and then you took them from me
and I remember coming home to find folded up pages
that you'd torn from my diary
and once when I tried to take them back
you told me they were already photocopied,
that you'd given them to the pastors to read
and all I could do was just scream unintelligibly
because you had all of my words to hold against me
and I had nothing.
No, I'm not sorry for anything.
I used to hang from your words like they were monkey bars
stretching across the stars
in the handle of the Big Dipper, leading me North.
But they stopped short,
unable to support me
and I went plummeting.
You gave me words, but they were worthless
and sometimes I find myself waiting for dementia to settle in
so you will forget my sin,
so I can be your baby and lay my head on your heart again
and we can just be.
And I'll take your hand and lay it on my chest
so you can feel the rhythm of my life
and maybe in that place
beyond stars and space,
you'll finally be able to really see me,
and truly love me completely unconditionally.

I remember climbing high
into our aging silver maple

with no map to climb back down,
leaping over muddy, rushing creeks
and hoping to fall in.
I remember tackle football grass stains
skidded onto the chests of my t-shirts,
running full-speed at my big brother
after being taunted and knowing full well
he was going to bring up that knee,
throw me down and pummel me.
I remember swingset kicking a sky
so blue it almost hurt my eyes,
speeding downhill on my bike
with arms stretched out wide,
the wind stealing the breath from my lungs,
and I felt powerful,
like anything was possible.
And I didn't yet know the difference
between being fearless and being brave.

Rambo Renegades

When I was young I was proud of the bruises on my legs,
of the dirt stains on my plain white T-Shirts.
When I was young I was so damn proud of that denim
vest I bought from target with my own money,
the closest I could get to that Outsiders look.
When I was young, I wanted to be a greaser,
a Rambo renegade, a street rat with a heart of gold.
When I was young my brother used to run inside yelling,
"Ma-ahhhhm! Rachel's playing Aladdin again
and she's not wearing a shirt under her vest!"
When I was young I used to draw pictures of shirtless men
with muscular contoured chests.
When I was young I wanted to be a boy
because I thought only boys could be strong.
When I was young my brother used to hold me down
and sometimes the look in his eye would scare me.
Sometimes I can still feel him holding my biceps down with his knees,
hear his words from between gritted teeth, "Open your mouth.
Open your mouth!" and when I finally did, he spit.
When I was young I went to the gym with my mother one day
and I thought that when I got home, I'd have big muscles,
that I'd be stronger than my brother and I couldn't wait
to see the look on his face.
When we got to the gym I went straight for the free weights.
I stood at the rack in front of the mirror and watched my grin fade
as I realized that only the smallest ones weren't too heavy for me

and after only a few badly formed curls
even those were too much for me
and I quickly realized that changing your body
isn't done quite so easily
and on the car ride home I cried with my face to the window
and couldn't quite put a name to what I was feeling.
When I was young I wanted to be a boy
because I wanted to have a girlfriend.
I wanted to believe in the fantasies
birthed from movie and television sex scenes.
I wanted to feel a woman's body beneath me
and when I realized that, in my world, that wasn't a possibility
I cried with my face in my pillow
and I couldn't quite put a name to what I was feeling.
And I was young, younger than ten
the first time I cut myself on purpose
and I could stand up here right now
and show you all of the scars that I gave to myself
when I thought that in order to be seen as strong,
you had to prove that you'd been through battle
and I'd been through battle,
I just wanted the evidence to be physical,
my toughness to be visible.
And isn't it funny how these scars just made me look weak,
like I needed someone to save me
and maybe I just needed someone to save me
from the misguided belief that strength is tied to masculinity
and that masculinity is tied to maleness.
Maybe I just needed someone to save me from my adolescent penis envy
because now that I'm older I know that you don't have to be a man
to fuck a woman.

That fucking a woman doesn't mean she's beneath you.

That fucking a woman shouldn't make you feel strong,

like you've risen higher in the hierarchy.

Now that I'm older I can address my own misogyny.

Now that I'm older I love being a woman.

I love being a woman that loves other women.

And there is nothing like being inside of a woman

when she is inside of me, that mutual ecstasy.

Now that I'm older I can finally put a name

to all of those confused feelings,

because I've realized that all I've ever wanted

was just the freedom to be me

and now that I've claimed that liberty,

I find I'm just waiting for equality.

Now that I'm older, I don't want to be strong

in order to hold my brother down.

I don't want to hold any of my brothers down.

I just want us to stand hand in hand

and maybe together we can show the

next generation of young women

that they can be whatever they want to be,

that there is a strength inside of them

that the world is waiting to see,

that they are Rambo renegades

and they don't have to change a thing.

Dust Bowl

I think about the dust bowl a lot.
About those who chose to stay.
About the crows who built their nests
with coils of barbed wire
when straw became scarce,
and there was no grass to be found.
I think about the mothers
with black creased brows,
the damp pinks of their lungs
coated in a fine gray silt.
The ones who
stuffed their sills with linens,
who leaned blindly
into winds heavy with dark.
I think about the crows cradled against
all that unforgiving sharpness.
I think about their eggs.
I think about the men
who found those nests,
who took photos of the wonder.
The fathers with so much condemned Earth
tucked between their angry teeth,
they had no choice but to go on
tonguing the massive grit
of their last, yawning mistake.

When I think about the dust bowl
and the ones who stayed
I wonder if I should
admire their strength
or admonish their stubbornness.
I wonder if it is possible
to measure the weight
of manifest destiny
in dirt.

When I think about the dust bowl
and the ones who stayed,
I think about my mother,
the ones I left behind
at a condemned Riverside.
The church.
The cult that raised me.
I think about my mother.
Still there, always there.
Hunched over her burgundy chair,
bible open, lips trembling
with a prayer that is less
words than weeping.
Mascara staining wadded tissues
stuffed into cracks and pressed completely flat
by the weight of the old testament.
Creased eyes bleeding black,
my empty nest mother

my empty nest mother
hunched over her barbed wire chair
and plowing up a storm.
Crying out our names
to a cloudless gray sky.
A black blizzard behind her on the horizon,
I see her standing there
in the open plain.
Believing in the lie of the harvest.
Praying for her prodigals to return.
And waiting,
always,
for the rain.

On Breaking Clouds

My mother used to tell me I was too clumsy for my own
good,
that I never paid attention to my surroundings.
But maybe I wanted to tornado myself
through our fragile home
like the storm of words that broke
so many hopes inside of me.
Maybe I should apologize
to all of the small things
that I broke
in order to feel powerful:
Every crayon in the pencil box
when I was three years old
just because I could
and it felt good.
The countless sticks
I cracked against the trunks of towering
silver maples when I wanted to feel
as free as their dancing leaves.
My mother's heart
when I was nineteen
and I just wanted to be me.
Sometimes my tornado is a ghost that gets away from me.
And some things are made to be broken
like hollow sticks
and mothers' hearts
and sometimes "I'm sorry"
is the gentle rain
after my storm
and sometimes
there is no sorry at all,
just silence
and debris.

Writer's Block

My ex sends me poems from Asia,
foreign cities in their titles,
a nameless boy she writes about in second person,
but the poems aren't about him,
just like they weren't about me.
Not really.

It's been five years since she skipping stone
flitted over oceans,
since she medusa-ed me
into putting on a brave mountain face.
Except I've always been softer than I'd hoped.
Skin, hips, heart.
When she left me
I wrote a song about Whiskey.

And even five years later,
those yous, this nameless muse,
shoot through my breastplate,
dropping my heart just barely,
just a few centimeters,
but I'm surprised by the weight
she still bears on me.

Five years later.
Oceans away.
And this is the first poem
I've written in months.

Waterslide

The screensaver on my phone
is a child's drawing of a twisting slide
with giant spikes at the bottom.
And in adorable elementary handwriting, the words
"Life's a waterslide where you die at the end."
On the slide is a depiction of the life cycle,
starting with a baby at the top and an old man with a cane
flying up off the bottom suspended in mid air above the giant spikes.

This is my screensaver for two reasons.
One, it's fucking hilarious.
I laugh every time I see it.
Did I mention it has the words "you are here"
with an arrow pointing to the empty space
just before the old man flying off the end?
I can only hope that this was a birthday card
to this savage kid's aging grandfather.
What a dick!
The second reason I have this picture as my screensaver:
It terrifies me.
It tightens my chest
and drops my stomach.
It ruins my fucking day.
A constant reminder of my own mortality.
The absurdity of life and death
right there in the crude 2-D drawing
of some nine-year-old asshole.

A brilliant metaphor
that captures the root
of my enormous fear of death.
The lack of control.
Have you ever tried to climb up a waterslide?
I have.
It was a stone waterslide in Costa Rica.
Late at night and we had the pool to ourselves.
My friend and I were topless
and tripping on acid
and we dared each other to try.
It did not end well.
Because climbing a water slide
while tripping on acid is almost completely impossible.
And in the metaphorical waterslide of life
it's always impossible.
You don't start in the pool.
There is no fucking pool.
Only giant spikes, remember?!?!
There's no going back up,
no chance to catch your breath,
get your bearings,
form any semblance of a grip.
You're flung down
without ever being asked
if you even wanted
to go down this hellslide
in the first place
and it's all happening so fast

and the water is pushing you
and rushing around you
and over your head
and you're twisting
and turning;
and gravity,
the weight of your own body,
your continued velocity,
is forcing you downward ever faster,
and it's going so fast
and where the fuck does it end, though?
Like, I know it's going to end!
I know the spikes are down there!
But how long is the fucking slide?!
And how bad is this gonna hurt?
And what happens after?
And why can't I be in control?!
And someone give me another Fucking hit of acid!
And oh fuck, dear god, why can't I be in control?!?!

Most often my suicidal thoughts
aren't because I'm depressed,
because I hate life
and want to die.

It's because I love life.
And I don't want death to rob that from me
in some absurd way
at whichever absurd moment it chooses.
I want to be in charge.

I want to say when it's over
and how.
I want everything to have meaning.
But it doesn't.
And when I unlock my phone
I'm reminded of my mortality,
of existential absurdity.
I'm reminded that god
is basically a nine year old dick with a crayon.

And also that waterslides
are fucking fun as hell.
Even when they're scary.
Especially when they're scary.
And when I'm finally flung off the bottom,
and plummeting toward those giant spikes
and about to be impaled,
I'll be flailing and screaming,
but I'm pretty sure
I'll also be laughing.

Made in the USA
San Bernardino, CA
14 July 2018